David Davies

EL GRECO

PHAIDON
Oxford

E.P. DUTTON
New York

Acknowledgements

I am especially indebted to Mrs Enriqueta Frankfort, Professor Sir Anthony Blunt and Professor Sir Ellis Waterhouse, without whose help and encouragement this book would not have been written. I also wish to thank Gregorio de Andrés and Angel M. García Gómez in whose company I have spent endless profitable and pleasurable hours. I have also benefited greatly from discussions with Professors A. A. Parker and the late R. O. Jones, J. Cummins, B. Tate, J. Varey and X. de Salas; Dr D. P. Walker, Dr C. Schmidt, Mr B. A. R. Carter and Mr A. Lucas. I am grateful to the Winston Churchill Memorial Trust, the Arts Faculty of University College and the Central Research Fund of the University of London for generous financial aid and to Professor J. White for his unfailing moral support.

D.D.

The publishers are grateful to the museums and church authorities who have given permission to reproduce the paintings in their possession, and especially to Señora M. Blanch of Ampliaciones y Reproducciones Mas for her most generous help. *The Assumption of the Virgin* (Plate 1) is reproduced by courtesy of the Art Institute of Chicago.

Phaidon Press Limited, Littlegate House, St Ebbe's Street, Oxford
Published in the United States of America by E. P. Dutton & Co., Inc.

First published 1976
© *1976 by Elsevier Publishing Projects SA Lausanne/Smeets Illustrated Projects, Weert*

ISBN 0 7148 1740 6
Library of Congress Catalog Card Number: 76-1346

Printed in the Netherlands

EL GRECO

'There has arrived in Rome a young Candiot pupil of Titian who in my judgement is exceptional in painting . . .' (Giulio Clovio to Cardinal Alessandro Farnese, 16 November 1570). The young painter was Domenicos Théotocopoulos, called El Greco. He was born in Candia on the island of Crete, then a Venetian possession, and is recorded there as a master painter in 1566. It is significant that he used gold in a picture of the *Passion of Christ*, reflecting his training in the traditional techniques of Byzantine painting.[1] Two years later he was in Venice; while there he worked in Titian's studio. On his arrival in Rome he probably stayed at the Farnese Palace and in 1572 became a member of the Academy of St. Luke. It is conceivable that he returned to Venice before going to Spain. He visited Madrid, possibly to obtain commissions from Philip II to paint pictures for the Escorial. In 1577 he went to the former imperial city, Toledo, in order to paint the altarpieces for the church of Santo Domingo el Antiguo and remained there until his death.

'He was a great philosopher, shrewd in his remarks, and he wrote on painting, sculpture, and architecture,' wrote Francisco Pacheco (*Arte de la Pintura*, Seville 1649). Although his treatises are lost, El Greco's interest in philosophy, theology, literature and history is reflected in the inventory of his library[2] and in those intellectuals whose company he frequented in Italy and Spain. Among those residing in the Farnese Palace when El Greco was in Rome were Fulvio Orsini, antiquarian and librarian (who commissioned pictures from El Greco); Matteos Devaris, who translated into Greek the Decrees of the Council of Trent; Pedro Chacón, the Toledan employed to reform the Gregorian Calendar.[3] In Spain he was associated with the Augustinian[4] and Franciscan[5] Orders. He was in close contact with the historian Pedro de Salazar y Mendoza, the clerics Luis and Diego de Castilla (the latter was Dean of Toledo Cathedral), the antiquarian Antonio de Covarrubias, and the poet and lawyer Dr Gregorio Angulo.[6] It is likely that he was acquainted with others of their circle: the distinguished Augustinian poet and writer Luis de León;[7] the celebrated blind organist Francisco Salinas;[8] the biblical scholar and librarian of the Escorial, Benito Arias Montano;[9] the enlightened archbishop of Toledo, Cardinal Gaspar de Quiroga.[10] His praises were sung by Góngora and Hortensio Paravicino, the Trinitarian poet and court preacher. These men undoubtedly tempered his intellectual outlook and so had a profound bearing on his evolution as an artist. As Paravicino commented, 'Crete gave him life and Toledo his brushes.' Indeed, El Greco's handling of light, colour and form reveals a specific philosophical concept – Neoplatonism – which reflects his response to the spiritual climate of Toledo at the time of the Catholic Reformation.

At the time of El Greco's arrival Toledo must have presented a scene of intense religious activity. Already in 1537 Alejo Venegas, in his *Agonía del tránsito de la muerte*, had described it as a city 'where the sanctity of the Church automatically invites him [a Catholic] to live in a saintly manner! Over and above the great number of the clergy and the multitude of monasteries of all the religious orders . . . there are confraternities of the devout in this city so numerous that one would think that all such organizations in all of Spain had gathered for a convention in Toledo.'[11] It was propitious that in the year of El Greco's arrival, Gaspar de

Quiroga was appointed Archbishop. Like his predecessor, Bartolomé Carranza, he pursued a policy that reflected the best ideals of Tridentine catholicism. He supervised the publication in 1581 of a manual of the Sacraments; the following year he convoked a Council of Toledo in order to encourage the reform of the clergy and to implement the decrees of the Council of Trent.[12] It would seem that El Greco not only responded to the spirit of this reform movement but was also fully aware of the doctrinal significance of the Decrees: he owned a Greek translation of the Decrees; he was an intimate friend of Antonio Covarrubias, a former legate at the Council of Trent;[13] the subject-matter of his paintings is in accord with the new teaching of the Catholic Reformation – the Purification of the Temple, the Martyrdom of Saints, the contemplation of death, and acts of Penitence and Charity.[14]

In contrast to the bigotry and conservatism of some contemporary religious bodies, Quiroga seems to have encouraged an atmosphere in which intellectual and speculative thinking could flourish. It would appear that, like Erasmus, he championed scholarship as a prerequisite of moral instruction. As Inquisitor General he protected Francisco Salinas and that group of eminent biblical scholars, Luis de León, Arias Montano and Francisco Sánchez el Brocense[15] – all of whom were intimates of the men associated with El Greco. Together with El Greco's patrons, Diego de Castilla and Pedro de Salazar y Mendoza, Quiroga staunchly supported the reputation of Bartolomé Carranza, who had suffered the ignominy of the Inquisition on account of his Erasmist tendencies.[16] Possibly it was Quiroga who quashed the niggling criticism of El Greco's *Espolio;*[17] certainly he gave his approval for the painting of that most novel subject, the *Burial of the Count of Orgaz*.[18]

Moreover, Quiroga[19] and Diego de Covarrubias[20] were sympathetic to a spiritual movement which was characterized by the quest for direct communion of the soul with God through contemplation – a movement that was to have a profound influence on the art of El Greco. In Spain this striving after spiritual renovation had originated in the time of Cisneros and was subsequently encouraged by the followers of Erasmus. Not only did they protest against clerical abuses, they also sought to establish a society dominated by an ideal of Christian piety. But by the mid-sixteenth century the Erasmian movement had lost favour officially and some of the writings of Erasmus were banned.[21] Nevertheless, these ideals were also pursued within the reformed religious orders and in the last four decades of the sixteenth century found their finest literary expression in the spiritual writings of Luis de León, Luis de Granada, St. John of the Cross and St. Teresa.[22]

An important facet of this movement was the emphasis on Christological spirituality.[23] This was given doctrinal support by the Tridentine Decrees relating to Grace. In addition, the celebration of the Sacraments now became a daily occurrence in the life of the priesthood.[24] Thus the priest was made constantly aware that he was in the presence of the real, the physical Christ. It is noteworthy that El Greco eventually rejects narrative scenes with didactic content in favour of images which reveal the mysteries of the Faith or which concentrate on the spiritual significance of Christ and his saints.

Another important aspect of this spiritual movement was the profound interest in Neoplatonism.[25] This provided an intellectual framework with its concept of the subordination of the physical world to the world of the spirit, that higher reality to which man aspired. It would seem that, with the gradual erosion of Erasmian influence, the spiritual writers derived increasing intellectual support from Neoplatonism. It is generally true that this interest was particularly characteristic of the Augustinian and Franciscan orders,[26] with which El Greco was associated.

One of the most influential Neoplatonic sources, to which the spiritual writers constantly referred, was Pseudo-Dionysius the Areopagite.[27] He claimed to be the Dionysius who was converted to Christianity after hearing St. Paul preach on the Areopagus at Athens, but he is now thought to have been an anonymous Syrian theologian living about A.D. 500. His treatises were generally regarded in the sixteenth century as second only to the Gospels and were cited by many of El Greco's contemporaries: the Augustinians, Luis de León,[28] the Blessed Alonso de Orozco[29], who founded the Colegio de Dona María de Aragon and Cristóbal de Fonseca[30], who dedicated a Neoplatonic treatise to a member of that branch of the Mendoza family which regarded itself as descended from the Lord of Orgaz; the Carmelite, St. John of the Cross[31], and Francisco de Quiroga,[32] the nephew of Cardinal Quiroga.

The reverence accorded to Pseudo-Dionysius in Toledo is of special significance. Owing to the controversy over the Primacy of Toledo, it was felt expedient to bring the relics of St. Eugenius from the abbey church of St. Denis, on the outskirts of Paris, to Toledo. The importance of St. Eugenius was not simply that he had been the first archbishop of Toledo but that, according to legend, he had been a convert of St. Dionysius.[33] One of the organizers of the translation of the relics in 1565 was Diego de Castilla[34], the future patron of El Greco.

In one of the most important treatises written by the Pseudo-Dionysius, the *Celestial Hierarchy*, the Divine was interpreted in terms of light metaphysics. Radiant light emanates from God; it is imparted to angels who 'abide in Heaven, where Light is; and . . . they impart wholly intelligible Light and are enlightened intellectually'.[35] They transmit it from one to the other in descending order, that is, through the celestial hierarchy. Ultimately the Divine Light spiritually illuminates the mind of man. He, in turn, with the help of angels, can ascend the hierarchy from the physical to the Divine. Initially he needs to contemplate the physical world which will provide a stepping-stone to the Divine: 'the earthly lights [are] a figure of the immaterial enlightenment.'[36]

It is significant that a Greek edition of the *Celestial Hierarchy* figures in the 1614 inventory of El Greco's library.[37] Moreover, El Greco affirms his belief in its concept of light metaphysics in the inscription on his *View and Plan of Toledo* (see notes to Plate 40), in which he refers to the Virgin and angels in the language of Pseudo-Dionysius as celestial bodies and implies in this conceit that they emit light.

Also in the story of Our Lady who gives the Chasuble to St Ildefonso, for their adornment and in order to make the figures large I have availed myself of the fact that they are celestial bodies as we can see in the case of lights which, seen from afar, appear large however small they may be.

When El Greco translated these concepts into his religious paintings he clearly had recourse to Pseudo-Dionysius's favourite symbol for angels – fire.

. . . I think that this image of fire signifies the perfect conformity to God of the Celestial Intelligences . . . It illuminates them all with its resplendent brightness. It is . . . uplifting . . . it suddenly enkindles its light . . . uncontrollably flying upwards without diminishing its all blessed self-giving.[38]

The image of fire was not only one of the most common in contemporary spiritual literature,[39] it was also cited in artistic theory. Giovanni Paolo Lomazzo refers to the flame of fire in the section on Proportion in Book I of his *Trattato dell' arte della pittura* (1584) (possibly the item referred to in the inventory of El Greco's library as *Tratado de la Pintura*): 'For the greatest grace and life, that a picture can have, is, that is expresse 'Motion': which the Painters call the 'spirite' of a picture: Nowe there is no forme so fitte to expresse this 'Motion', as that of the flame of fire . . . for it hath a 'Conus' or sharpe pointe wherewith it seemeth to divide the aire, that so it may ascende to his proper sphere.' (Haydock translation.) The image of the flame is synonymous not only with brightness but with elongation of form. In this context it is noteworthy that in the contract for the decoration of the Oballe Chapel (Plate 44), El Greco increased the original designs of the deceased Alexandro Seminaio by more than one fifth 'and in this manner the fabric achieves perfect form'.[40]

It is not known whether El Greco had assimilated the concepts of Neoplatonism before going to Spain but it would seem that from the 1580s his handling of light, colour and form is intended to express Christian doctrine according to these concepts and that his work may only be fully understood by reference to them. He rejected the notion of seeing the manifestation of God solely in naturalistic forms and utilized the conceptual forms of Mannerist art as an aid to the contemplation of God. The dazzling brightness of his light and colour is intended to be a reflection of Divine Light which will illuminate the mind of the beholder. The soaring movement from naturalistically described forms to heavenly beings of superhuman proportions will enable the soul of the beholder to ascend to God. Even when the naturalistic device is not employed, the idea is always present because the distortion of colour, light, form and space in the painting vividly impresses upon the beholder the contrast with the physical nature of his own existence. The function of El Greco's religious paintings, like the spiritual poems of Luis de León, is to raise the soul of man heavenwards with its movement of spirit.

In contrast to this mature style El Greco's early work in Italy reveals his concern with naturalistic representation. His painting of the *Purification of the Temple* (Plate 2) is a bold but abortive attempt to emulate the achievements of High Renaissance painters. The design resembles that of Michelangelo's drawings of the subject; many of the figures are derived from Michelangelo, Raphael and Titian; the rhythmic outlines of the forms suggest the influence of Tintoretto, while the iridescent colours and flickering highlights are reminiscent of both Tintoretto and Bassano. But the composition is loosely organized, the treatment of space confused, the drawing imprecise and the painting is overloaded with iconographic paraphernalia.

Under the impact of the works in Rome of Michelangelo and Raphael, his painting of the second version of the *Purification of the Temple* (Plate 3) reveals a more stable design, space is better articulated, the structure of forms is more accurately rendered. But his sensibility to colour and his handling of paint – the use of glazes, scumbles and impasto swept over a fairly coarsely woven canvas – are a debt to his Venetian training, particularly in Titian's workshop.

This naturalistic style reaches its climax in his earliest works in Toledo: the altarpieces for Santo Domingo el Antiguo (1577–79) and the *Espolio* (1577–79) painted for the Cathedral. In the former, he adapted Vignola's design for the façade of the Gesú in Rome to the entire architectural framework of the retable in the Capilla Mayor, thereby imposing on the native Plateresque tradition a grander sense of scale and a clearer disposition of all the canvases. This sense of grandeur and clarity is echoed in the central canvas, the *Assumption of the Virgin* (Plate 1), in which the symmetry of the design is sustained by colour. Primary colours –

the yellow light and the red and blue drapery of the Virgin – accentuate the central axis. Complementary greens are placed at the lower margins. Pink, yellow and purplish grey are balanced diagonally across the surface. The chromatic brilliance of such effects is enhanced by the bright light shining on broad areas of form. Forms are three-dimensional, sharply delineated and aligned with others in different spatial planes so that all appear to be fused into the surface plane, thus creating the illusion that they project into the space of the beholder. The illusion is heightened by relating the gaze of the Virgin and the direction of light in the painting to the source of real light in the Capilla Mayor, streaming down from the windows above.

This desire to convince the beholder that he is a witness to a real event is conspicuous in the *Espolio* (the disrobing of Christ before the Crucifixion) (Plate 9). By means of precise drawing and smoother handling of paint El Greco created convincing three-dimensional forms. They are conceived from a close viewpoint and compressed, like cut-outs, into such a shallow space as to suggest high-relief polychrome sculpture. The beholder is face to face with a raucous, jostling crowd while the executioner bores a hole in the Cross, which seems to lie at the feet of the beholder. But this claustrophobic space, with its grim foreboding of death, is disrupted by the majestic figure of Christ. His physical power is expressed by the device of dual viewpoints and emphasized by the axial symmetry of the design. But it is colour rather than drawing or design which reveals his divinity. The scarlet robe, intensified by the adjacent yellows, gleams like a jewel, reassuring the beholder of the triumph of Christ.

During the 1580s, El Greco developed a style which is characterized by colours that are more expressive and less descriptive. There is an increasing use of black, white and sulphur-yellow. Tonal transitions from light to dark are distinct. Forms are flatter, more elongated and compressed into shallow spatial planes that are occasionally juxtaposed to create dramatic changes of scale. The whole is woven into a pattern of rhythmic curves. Renaissance rules of perspective and proportion have been rejected. The physical world is increasingly subordinated to the spiritual.

These characteristics are already evident in the *Crucifixion* (Plate 12). Although the original setting is not known, the painting probably rested directly on an altar. The priest and donor are naturalistically portrayed and are shown at the base of the painting, on the same eye-level as the living priest standing at the altar. Thus the device of the stepping-stone from the physical to the supernatural is repeated, as in the *Resurrection* (see note to Plate 13). But here the portrayal of the supernatural in naturalistic terms has been abandoned. The flattening and elongation of Christ's body and the zig-zag pattern of clouds tinged with flickering, incandescent light create the impression that the priest and donor are no longer witnessing a real event. They contemplate the spiritual significance of his death.

El Greco's most distinguished essay in this style is the *Burial of the Count of Orgaz* (1586–8) (Plate 14). It is also one of his earliest interpretations of the destiny of man according to Neoplatonic concepts of cosmic hierarchy, illumination and the ascent of the soul. The picture commemorates the burial in 1323 of the Lord of Orgaz, a benefactor of the Church of Santo Tomé, when Saints Augustine and Stephen miraculously appeared and placed the deceased in his sepulchre. The miraculous vision is conjured up by an astonishing handling of colour and light. The opaque blacks melt into the shadows of the dark chapel, suppressing corporality; the transparent whites, greens and grey-blues evoke an ethereal atmosphere. The combination of dazzling whites, pale yellows and rich gold gives the painting a hieratic quality that is emphasized by the formalism of the two-dimensional design. The whole is reminiscent of those Byzantine images of the Dormition of the Virgin which, as a Cretan, he must have known. The physical reality is vividly expressed in such naturalistic details as the Count's damascened armour glinting in the gloom, the richly embroidered vestments of the Saints and the diaphanous surplice of the priest. The illusion of reality is heightened by the device whereby the beholder is to be imagined standing in front of the tomb (originally represented in fresco beneath the canvas but subsequently lost) and by the presence of contemporary Toledans. But their sharply lit, serried heads create a pattern of restless energy. They hover between the natural world and the supernatural. They are not only witness to a miracle, they are momentarily transfixed by its mystery.

Above their heads, an angel bearing the soul of the Count in the insubstantial form of a child swirls heavenwards. As there is no reference in the contract for the painting[41] either to the angel or to the soul of the Count, in spite of detailed instructions as to the painting of the actual burial scene, their inclusion reveals El Greco's interest in the nature of the soul, its ascent from the body to heaven and the role of angels as guides to the Divine. The celestial vision is characterized by the elongation of the figures, the schematic treatment of clouds and drapery, which are reduced to almost two-dimensional patterns, and the exceedingly bright light emanating from Christ which cascades down on to the glacial clouds and flashes across the zig-zag folds of drapery. No longer the embodiment of physical beauty as in the Resurrection, Christ is now conceived of as a radiance of light.

In the years that follow, El Greco's style gains in intensity. He abandons foreshortening in favour of two-dimensional patterns. He clearly makes no reference to the life model, a fact which would seem to be confirmed by his use of wax, plaster and clay models. The elongation of the figures with their relatively small heads is more exaggerated so that they assume flame-like shapes. Similarly, the format of his paintings becomes increasingly vertical. Light is more intense and seems to emanate individually from each form. There is a greater variety of colour, colours are brighter and are distinct from one another:

'Who will believe that Dominico Greco returned to his paintings many times and that he retouched them time and again so as to leave the colours distinct and separate . . .'[42] The juxtaposition of the colours causes them to vibrate and it is this rather than the drawing that creates the illusion of relief:

'. . . we see some things painted by his [El Greco's] hand so full of relief and life-like (in that style of his) that they equal those of the greatest men . . .'[43] Such effects were given added force by El Greco's drastic simplification of the traditional Venetian method of oil glazing. Instead of superimposing glazes (that is, transparent pigment) over layers of opaque pigment, he generally applied oil glazes in varying thicknesses directly on to the underpainting. Thus the glowing modulations of colour, which he had learnt from Titian, have been abandoned in favour of startling contrasts and harsher brilliance. This direct method of painting is coupled with a decorative use of broken colour. There is no attempt to convey the appearance of form in space by observing the colour changes within that form or its interrelationship with adjacent colours. His pictures in this final phase are not, like the late works of Titian, essays in atmospheric painting. El Greco transcends physical reality and creates an illusion of brightly burning images suspended in infinite space. This effect is heightened by contours which lack clear definition and which seem to release light and colour from their confines. Thus the two-dimensional design characteristic of the 1580s is disrupted by the vertical thrust of forms and the outburst of incandescent light and brilliant colour: an effect akin to the immediacy of revelation encountered in contemporary spiritual literature.

His supreme skill and the conceptual handling of colour, light and form are evident in his portraiture as well as in his religious compositions. His portrait of the Inquisitor General, Cardinal Fernando Niño de Guevara (Plate 25), has the trappings of a splendid state portrait with its backcloth of rich brocade and with its dazzling light flashing across stiff folds of sumptuous watered-silk. But the acidic colours, compressed spatial planes and taut, sharp-edged contours create a tense atmosphere. It is heightened by the contrast between the rigid position of Guevara's head and the agitated outlines of drapery which flow into the pattern of the brocade, creating restless elliptical shapes. Guevara has let slip a piece of paper, ironically bearing El Greco's signature. He seems to fidget in his chair, his feet askew. His expression is furtive and uneasily he grips one arm of the chair.

El Greco's ability to transcend physiognomy and evoke the spirit of the man is beautifully recorded in his sympathetic portrait of Hortensio Paravicino (Plate 33), the Trinitarian poet and court preacher. With consummate skill he conveys the sophistication and sensitivity of his friend by sweeping paint into a pattern of fluid, elegant shapes, abandoning the spatial tension and incisive linearity of the Guevara portrait. The exciting play between black and white never degenerates into a strident contrast: it is muted by brown, red and grey. It is not surprising that Paravicino was inspired to compose a sonnet in which he described El Greco as the 'Divine Greek' in whose work 'art surpasses reality'.[44]

El Greco's concern with the realm of the spirit is, perhaps, best conveyed in his decorative schemes for the Augustinian Colegio de Doña María de Aragón, Madrid (1596–1600) (Plates 20, 23), the Chapel of San José, Toledo (1597–99) (Plate 22), the Hospital of La Caridad, Illescas (1603–5) (Plates, 31, 34, 35), the Oballe Chapel in San Vicente, Toledo (1607–13) (Plates 43, 44) and the Hospital of San Juan Bautista Extra Muros, Toledo (begun in 1608 and completed after Greco's death by his son Jorge Manuel) (Plate 48). The *Immaculate Conception* from the Oballe Chapel in San Vicente is possibly the most splendid example. Originally the painting rested on the altar. At the bottom of the canvas there is a cluster of lilies and roses (symbols of the Virgin) naturalistically rendered as if to mirror real flowers placed on the altar.[45] Elsewhere in the painting El Greco has distorted light, colour and form; heavenly beings of immense scale soar effortlessly heavenwards; garments of bright blue and red and yellow are juxtaposed to create a psychedelic effect while dazzling light is reflected off these garments with such intensity that each seems to have its own source of light. From naturalistic flowers a vision of heavenly beings flares upwards illuminating the dark night.

> O lamps of burning fire
> In whose translucent glow
> The mind's profoundest caverns shine with splendour
> Before in blindness and obscure,
> With unearthly beauty now
> Regale their love with heat and light together.
> (St John of the Cross, *The Living Flame of Love*)[46]

The inclusion of naturalistic details at the bottom of the painting thus provides the beholder with a stepping-stone from the 'sensible to the intelligible',[47] that is, to the realm of heavenly beings. He may continue his ascent with their aid until perhaps ultimately attaining union with God.

> For now we see through a glass darkly; but then face to face.
>
> (St Paul, I Corinthians, xiii. 12.)

To El Greco and the spiritual writers, life was dream; reality was transcendental.

El Greco's art may thus be seen as his response to a spiritual reform movement in Spain at the time of the Catholic Reformation. But although many of his pictures illustrate Catholic Reformation themes, his stylistic interpretation, especially after 1580, does not accord with that proposed at Trent and elaborated in subsequent artistic theory. The Tridentine insistence on clarity of presentation was to be reflected in the current emphasis on naturalism and on conformity to a set of rules. In his *Arte de la Pintura*, Francisco Pacheco (a censor for the Inquisition) gave detailed instructions as to how the 'Immaculate Conception of the Blessed Virgin Mary' should be naturalistically portrayed.[48] He found support for his approach in Aristotle's preference for verisimilitude over beautiful colours which bear no resemblance to the object depicted.[49] When Pacheco visited El Greco in 1611, it is not surprising that the latter expressed his disagreement with Aristotle's views on art.[50]

Moreover, El Greco eventually rejects narrative scenes with didactic emphasis in favour of images which reveal the spiritual significance of the Christian Faith. But this emphasis, which was common to El Greco and the spiritual writers, was to gain no sympathy from the established church with its increasing insistence on conformity and its hostility to speculative thinking. This is reflected in the growing antagonism to mysticism and the encouragement afforded to asceticism.[51] In the Jesuit Order, for example, the mystical experience of Ignatius Loyola, as recorded in his *Diario Espiritual*, was subordinated to the ascetic, active life he promulgated in the *Spiritual Exercises*. Indeed, the Jesuit confessor of St Teresa was commanded to return to the methods of the Exercises.[52] In the Dominican Order, the bastion of the Inquisition, there was considerable hostility towards Neoplatonism. Some argued that the Catholic faith was based on St Thomas Aquinas and that his doctrines were founded on Aristotle,[53] while Quevedo declared that Plato was a source of inspiration to heretics.[54]

Such rigid attitudes pervaded other forms of intellectual activity. The distinguished Jesuit, Juan de Mariana, who was a contemporary of El Greco in Toledo, wrote of the trial of Luis de León: 'The case in question disheartened many, as they saw the danger to others and the torment which threatened those who freely stated what they thought.' (*Pro Editione Vulgata*, 1609).

El Greco's attitude to the prevailing mood of increasing intolerance and conformity may well be reflected in his painting of Laocoön (Plate 41). Is it not possible to see in this painting an allegory of the destruction by the Inquisition of the former archbishop of Toledo, Bartolomé Carranza, a champion of the reform movement? As this priest of Toledo writhes in agony on the ground, the wooden horse trots towards the Visagra Gate. The sky is ominous and Toledo, as Carranza had preached, seems doomed. (See note to Plate 41).

It was not surprising that the art of El Greco had no successors. In spite of its aesthetic appeal, its significance could be grasped only by a sophisticated audience well-versed in spiritual literature and Neoplatonic concepts. As Hortensio Paravicino aptly remarked: 'Future ages will admire his genius but none will imitate it.'

Notes to the text

1. M. Constantoudaki, *Thesaurismata*, vol. XXII, 1975, p. 296ff.

2. F. de B. de San Román, *El Greco en Toledo* (Madrid, 1910), pp. 195–7; idem, 'De la vida del Greco', *Archivo Español de Arte y Arqueología*, III, *1927, pp. 306–309.*

3. *Pierre de Nolhac, La Bibliothèque de Fulvio Orsini* (Paris, 1887).

4. Gregorio de Andrés, 'El Greco y los Agustinos', *Revista del Colegio de Alfonso XII*, (1958–9), p. 12.

5. El Greco's numerous pictures of *St Francis* (approx. 25), the many more studio versions, as well as his work for the Colegio de San Bernardino, attest to his sympathy with Franciscan sentiment.

6. Harold E. Wethey, *El Greco and his School* (Princeton, 1962), vol. I., pp. 12–14.

7. A. F. G. Bell, *Luis de León* (Oxford, 1925), pp. 127, 134 n4, 150 n4.

8. Ibid., p. 131.

9. B. Rekers, *Benito Arias Montano* (London, 1972), pp. 60, 177.

10. A. Vegue Goldoni, 'El Cardenal Quiroga retratado por El Greco', *Archivo Español de Arte y Arqueología* (1928), p. 135. *See also* notes 16 and 17.

11. Otis H. Green, *Spain and the Western Tradition* (Madison and Milwaukee, 1965), vol. III, p. 148.

12. M. Boyd, *Cardinal Quiroga, Inquisitor General of Spain* (Dubuque, Iowa, 1954), ch. IV.

13. C. Gutiérrez, *Españoles en Trento* (Valladolid, 1951), p. 128ff.

14. E. Mâle, *L'Art Religieux de la fin du XVIe siècle, du XVIIe siècle et du XVIIIe siècle* (2nd ed., Paris, 1951); Ellis Waterhouse, 'Some Painters and the Counter-Reformation before 1600', *Transactions of the Royal Historical Society* (5th series, vol. XXII, 1972).

15. J. H. Elliott, *Imperial Spain 1469–1716* (London, 1963), p. 235.

16. See note to Plate 41.

17. El Greco was criticized because he had included the three Maries and had placed the crowd higher than Christ, but the picture remained unaltered. These objections would have been submitted to Quiroga, the Archbishop and Inquisitor General.

18. Wethey, op. cit., vol. II, p. 79.

19. J. Lynch, *Spain under the Habsburgs* (Oxford, 1965), vol. I, p. 252.

20. E. Allison Peers, *Saint Teresa of Jesus* (London, 1953), p. 40.

21. M. Bataillon, *Erasmo y España* (Mexico, 2nd ed., 1966), ch. I, IV, XI, XIII.

22. A. A. Parker, *The Spanish Mystics* (Open University Tape, No. A201. 26).

23. Ibid., Pedro Sáinz Rodríguez, Introduction to: Alain Guy, *El Pensamiento Filosófico de Fray Luis de León* (Madrid, 1960), p. 43.

24. H. Outram Evennett, *The Spirit of the Counter-Reformation* (Cambridge, 1968), p. 37.

25. A. A. Parker (oral communication); Elliott, op. cit., p. 237; Marcial Solana, *Historia de la Filosofía Española* (Madrid, 1941), vol. I. p. 686.

26. R. O. Jones, *The Golden Age: Prose and Poetry* (London, 1971), pp. 82–3, 106ff; E. Allison Peers, *Studies of the Spanish Mystics* (London, 1960), vol. III, p. 149.

27. Ibid., (Peers), vols. I–III, Indices 'Dionysius'.

28. Ibid., vol. I, (2nd ed.) p. 235ff.

29. Ibid., vol. II, p. 160.

30. Ibid., vol. II, p. 202. (*See also* note to Plate 14.)

31. Ibid., vol. III, pp. 26–7.

32. Ibid., vol. III, p. 50.

33. J. F. Rivera Recio, *San Eugenio de Toledo y su culto* (Toledo, 1963), p. 1, n2.

34. López de Ayala, *Toledo en el siglo XVI*

después del vencimiento de las comunidades (Madrid, 1901), p. 114, n63.

35. *Mystical Theology and the Celestial Hierarchies by Dionysius the Areopagite* (Shrine of Wisdom Press, Brook, 1965), p. 64.

36. Ibid., p. 22.

37. San Román, op. cit., p. 196. Rudolf Wittkower indicated that the rôle of the angels in the *Baptism* (Plate 48) is derived from this text ('El Greco's language of gesture', *Art News*, LVI, 1957 p. 45ff) See, also, p. 8 regarding the angel in the *Burial of the Conde de Orgaz*.

38. Dionysius, op. cit., p. 62.

39. Allison Peers, op. cit., vol. II, Index, 'fire'.

40. San Román, op. cit., p. 278.

41. Idem, pp. 142–6.

42. Pacheco, op. cit., Book III, ch. v.

43. Ibid., Book II, ch. x.

44. *Obras Posthumas divinas y humanas . . .* Madrid, 1641, folio 63.

45. Since it was stipulated in the contract that El Greco had to paint the picture 'with his own hand and not by another', this naturalistic detail is proof that his eyesight was not defective.

46. Gerald Brenan, *St John of the Cross*. (With a translation of the poetry by L. Nicholson) (Cambridge, 1973), p. 163.

47. Dionysius, op. cit., p. 22.

48. Pacheco, op. cit., Book III, ch. XI.

49. Ibid., Book I, XI.

50. Ibid., Book II, ch. XII.

51. Sáinz Rodríguez, op. cit., p. 58.

52. Outram Evennett, op. cit., pp. 65–6.

53. Bell, op. cit., p. 49ff.

52. 'Providencia de Dios', in *Obras en prosa*, ed. L. Astrana Marín (Madrid, 1932), pp. 1042–3.

The Plates

All pictures are painted in oil on canvas unless otherwise stated. Numbers in square brackets refer to catalogue entries in *El Greco and his School* (Princeton, 1962), vol. II, by Harold E. Wethey, which is of fundamental importance for the study of El Greco. In the following notes additional references are made only to those publications not cited by Wethey.

1. *The Assumption of the Virgin.* 1577. 401 × 229 cm. Chicago, Art Institute [1].
This was the central canvas of the high altar in Santo Domingo el Antiguo, Toledo, which was commissioned by Diego de Castilla, the Dean of the Cathedral.

2. *The Purification of the Temple.* About 1568–70. Tempera on panel, 65 × 83 cm. Washington, National Gallery of Art [104].
This subject acquired increasing importance during the Catholic Reformation because it was symbolic of the purging of the Church of heresy. It is illustrated on numerous papal medals of the period and there are many versions of it in El Greco's *oeuvre*. This early version (and that in Minneapolis) are literal interpretations of the Gospel according to St John.

3. *The Purification of the Temple.* About 1570–75. 117 × 150 cm. Minneapolis, Institute of Arts [105].
The portraits at lower right are an acknowledgement of El Greco's artistic sources. They are, from left to right, Titian, Michelangelo, Giulio Clovio and Raphael or, possibly, a self-portrait.

The presence of the child is possibly an allusion to Matthew xviii.3. 'Except ye be converted and become as little children, ye shall not enter the kingdom of heaven.' The glass chalice which is held by the child is probably a symbol of purification: at times of plague it was the practice to cleanse coins by dipping them in vinegar (e.g. Daniel Defoe, *A Journal of the Plague Year*, Everyman edition, p. 88).

4. *The Martyrdom of St Maurice.* 1580–2.

448 × 301 cm. Escorial, Nuevos Museos [265].

This was commissioned by Philip II for an altar dedicated to St Maurice in the basilica of the Escorial.

It was rejected and replaced by a painting by Ròmulo Cincinato. The latter depicted decapitated bodies spilling out of the picture in true orthodox fashion, whereas El Greco relegated the carnage to the background in favour of a 'disputa' on the theme of martyrdom.

5. *Allegory of the Holy League.* About 1576–8. Oil and tempera on panel, 58 × 35 cm. London, National Gallery [116].

This is a study for the larger and more refined version in the Escorial. It commemorates the victory of the Holy League over the Turks at the Battle of Lepanto in 1571 and refers to the destiny of the Christian Knight. The Church militant and the faithful kneel in adoration of the Name of Jesus; Hell is depicted by the jaws of Leviathan; Purgatory is represented by horsemen pushing sinners off a bridge into a burning pit.

6. Detail of Plate 4.

7. *Lady in a Fur Wrap.* About 1577–8. 62 × 50 cm. Glasgow, Pollok House [148].

8. Detail of Plate 4.

9. *El Espolio (The Disrobing of Christ).* 1577–9. 285 × 173 cm. Toledo, Cathedral Sacristy [78].

The facial expression and gestures of Christ recall the words which He spoke on the cross: 'Father, forgive them; for they know not what they do.' Luke xxiii.34. This novel treatment would seem to be El Greco's own invention.

10. Detail of Plate 9.

11. *St Peter in Tears.* About 1585–90. 106 × 88 cm. Barnard Castle, County Durham, Bowes Museum [269].

The subject refers to St Peter's denial of Christ (Matthew, xxvi. 75.) and the subsequent tradition, which is not recorded in the Gospels, that he shed tears of remorse every day of his life.

12. *The Crucifixion.* About 1580–5. 250 × 180 cm. Paris, Louvre [74].

Painted for the convent of the Jerónimas de la Reina, Toledo.

13. *The Resurrection of Christ.* 1577–9. 210 × 128 cm. Toledo, Santo Domingo el Antiguo [8].

This painting was commissioned for a side altar in the church of Santo Domingo el Antiguo, Toledo. It rests directly on the altar. At the bottom of the canvas, St Ildefonso is shown half length and wearing priest's vestments. He is on the same eye-level as (and consequently would have mirrored) the living priest standing at the altar. Thus the saint acts as intercessor and provides a stepping stone from the physical to the Divine, making the living priest a witness to the triumph of Christ.

14. *The Burial of the Count of Orgaz.* 1586–8. 480 × 360 cm. Toledo, Santo Tomé [123].

Is it not possible that the features of the dead man are those of the contemporary Conde de Orgaz? At that time the title had passed into a branch of the powerful Mendoza family (A.y.A. García Carraffa, *Enciclopedia Heráldica y Genealógica Hispano-Americana* vol. 40., p. 165ff). The family's desire to be associated with such an illustrious predecessor is reflected in the dedications of two treatises by the Augustinian Cristóbal de Fonseca: the *Primera parte de la Vida de Christo Señor nuestro*, Toledo, 1596 (this is dedicated to the Count of Orgaz, Juan de Mendoza y de Guzmán), the *Tratado del amor de Dios* Madrid, 1620 (this Neoplatonic treatise is dedicated to Francisco de Mendoza, Bishop of Salamanca).

15. Detail of Plate 14.

16. Detail of Plate 14.

17. *The Agony in the Garden.* About 1585–90. 102 × 114 cm. Toledo, Ohio, Museum of Art [29].

A startling variation on Titian's painting (or Giulio Bonasone's engraving after it), which was in Spain by 1574.

The pathetic figure of Christ seems to

be the source for Goya's frontispiece of *Los Desastres de la Guerra*.

18. Detail of Plate 14.
Portrait of Antonio de Covarrubias, Canon of the Cathedral, antiquarian and friend of El Greco.

19. *St Jerome as Cardinal*. About 1595–1600. 111 × 96 cm. New York, The Frick Collection [240].

20. *The Annunciation*. 1596–1600. 315 × 174 cm. Villanueva y Geltrú, Museo Balaguer [13].
It is generally agreed that this picture, together with *The Adoration of the Shepherds* (Bucharest) and *The Baptism of Christ* (Plate 23), originally formed part of the high altar of the Augustinian Colegio de Doña María de Aragón, Madrid.

21. Detail of Plate 20.

22. *St Martin and the Beggar*. About 1597–9. 193 × 103 cm. Washington D.C., National Gallery of Art [18].
This was originally a side altarpiece and formed part of El Greco's decoration of the Chapel of San José, Toledo.

23. *The Baptism of Christ*. 1596–1600. 350 × 144 cm. Madrid, Prado [14].
See note to Plate 20.

24. *St Francis and Brother Leo Meditating on Death*. About 1600–5. 168 × 103 cm. Ottawa, National Gallery of Canada [225]. Possibly painted for the Church of Cristo de las Aquas, Nambroca.

The image of a Saint meditating on death was common after the late sixteenth century, especially in Italy and Spain. The Jesuits, in particular, recommended the contemplation of a skull for this purpose. (Myron Laskin, Jr., *El Greco. St Francis and Brother Leo Meditating Death*, Ottawa, 1971.)

25. *Cardinal Fernando Niño de Guevara*. About 1600. 171 × 108 cm. New York, Metropolitan Museum of Art [152].
Probably painted in 1600–1 because Guevara came from Rome to Toledo early in 1600 as Inquisitor General and left the following year to take up the Archbishopric of Seville.

26. *The Crucifixion of Christ*. About 1600–5. 312 × 169 cm. Madrid, Prado [75]. Painted for the Jesuit church of San Ildefonso in Toledo. The idealized body of Christ and the profusion of his blood, which is enhanced by the preponderance of red in the picture, emphasize the significance of his sacrifice rather than his physical suffering.

27. *The Resurrection of Christ*. About 1600–5. 275 × 127 cm. Madrid, Prado [111]. Painted for Nuestra Señora de Atocha, Madrid. The soldiers with upraised arms and palms bent backwards are not threatening Christ but are acknowledging his divinity (Wittkower, op. cit., p. 45ff.). This same gesture of adoration is found in Roman art (Richard Brilliant, *Gesture and Rank in Roman Art*, New Haven, U.S.A., 1963, p. 16). The absence of the tomb suggests that El Greco is referring to the Christian tradition that the altar is a symbol of the tomb of Christ (John Shearman, *Pontormo's Altarpiece in S. Felicita*, Newcastle upon Tyne, 1971, p. 22.).

28. Detail of Plate 30.

29. *St Bernardino*. 1603. 269 × 144 cm. Toledo, Museo del Greco [200].
Painted for the high altar of the Franciscan Colegio de San Bernardino, Toledo.

30. *The Purification of the Temple*. About 1600. 106 × 130 cm. London, National Gallery [108].
The content of the painting is clarified by the bas-reliefs. The *Expulsion of Adam and Eve* is the Old Testament prototype of Sin and relates to the expulsion of the traders below. The *Sacrifice of Isaac* is a prefiguration of the Crucifixion and, therefore, a prototype of Redemption. This implies that the group below has been redeemed. Thus the female trader at the extreme right is to be interpreted as someone who, having sinned, has subsequently repented and is redeemed. 'In whom we have redemption through his blood, the forgiveness of sins, according to the riches of his grace', St Paul's 'Epistle to the Ephesians. i. 7.'

El Greco has integrated the doctrine of Redemption into the Gospel account of the Purification to transcend the narrative and reveal the spiritual illumination and purification of man.

Numerous *pentimenti* confirm Pacheco's account of El Greco's improvisation and indicate that the Frick version is later in date.

31. *The Coronation of the Virgin.* 1603–5. 163 × 220 cm. Illescas, Hospital de la Caridad [20].

Originally sited in the vault of the Capilla Mayor. Together with other paintings (e.g. Plates 34, 35) and statuary, it formed part of a unified decorative scheme which El Greco devised as a setting for a miraculous wooden image of the Madonna and Child.

No one painting has a consistent viewpoint. Nevertheless, all are designed to emphasize the wooden image with its cloak of real brocade in the centre of the altarpiece and to lead the eye upwards to the *Coronation* in the vault – an image of celestial bodies radiating Divine light. Only when the celebrant or communicant is at the entrance to the sanctuary are all these images visible and their purpose – the glorification of the Virgin – realized.

32. Detail of Plate 30.

33. *Fray Hortensio Félix Paravicino.* 1609. 113 × 86 cm. Boston, Museum of Fine Arts [153].

34. *St Ildefonso.* About 1603–5. 187 × 102 cm. Illescas, Hospital de la Caridad [23].

See note to Plate 31.

35. *The Madonna of Charity.* 1603–5. 184 × 124 cm. Illescas, Hospital de la Caridad [21].

See note to Plate 31.

36. *St Jerome in Penitence.* About 1610–14. 168 × 110 cm. Washington D.C., National Gallery of Art [249].

37. *The Vision of St John the Evangelist: The Fifth Seal of the Apocalypse.* 1608–14. 225 × 193 cm. New York, Metropolitan Museum of Art [120].

The subject is derived from Revelation vi, 9–11. The picture, of which the upper part has been destroyed, was probably intended for a side altar in the church of the Hospital of St John the Baptist Extra Muros, Toledo. (*See also* Plate 48.)

38. Detail of Plate 41.

39. *View of Toledo.* About 1595–1600. 121 × 109 cm. New York, Metropolitan Museum of Art [129].

This hymn to the forces of nature is paralleled in contemporary spiritual literature. Does it also imply, as in Luis de León's *Vida retirada*, that inner storm experienced by those who have not yet attained spiritual harmony? (Jones, op. cit., p. 103ff.)

40. *View and Plan of Toledo.* About 1610–14. 132 × 228 cm. Toledo, Museo del Greco [128].

In the sky the Virgin gives her chasuble to an angel, who will take it to St Ildefonso in the cathedral. This is barely discernible on the horizon below.

El Greco's observation about light (p. 5) is probably derived from a sixteenth-century edition of John Pecham's treatise on optics, the *Perspectiva Communis*: 'Firelight . . . appears larger from afar, since the distance makes it impossible to distinguish between the flame and the intense light near the flame, and so they are perceived by the eye undividedly as though a single great light.' (Proposition II). (D. C. Lindberg, *John Pecham and the Science of Optics*, London, 1970, p. 87).

El Greco has transformed a natural observation into a metaphysical conceit, implying that the Virgin and angels appear to be supernatural in size because they emit Divine Light.

In the inscription El Greco also explains that he placed the Hospital of St John the Baptist Extra Muros on a cloud because it obscured his view of the Visagra gate! Such a device is unusual in painting but was current in contemporary theatre where cloud-machines were frequently used. Indeed, he possessed a book on stage machinery: Jacques Besson, *Theatrum instrumentorum et machinarum*, Orleans, 1569.

A conceit is implicit here because hospitals were places where the welfare of the spirit was considered as important as that of the body. (Bartolomé de las Casas, *Opúsculos, Cartas y Memoriales*, Biblioteca de Autores Españoles, Madrid, 1958, vol. 110, p. 16.)

41. *Laocoön.* About 1610–14. 142 × 193 cm. Washington D.C., National Gallery of Art [127].

Laocoön was a priest of Troy who warned the Trojans of the Greek act of treachery in the form of the wooden horse. Subsequently two serpents came from the sea and killed Laocoön and his two sons. The choice of subject may have been inspired by an early tradition that Toledo was founded by two descendants of the Trojans, Telemon and Brutus. (Agapito Rey, *Sumas de Historia Troyana*, Madrid, 1932, p. 15.)

The picture may be an allegory of the destruction of Bartolomé Carranza. A priest of Toledo, he was appointed archbishop in 1558. In his first sermon at Toledo he gave warning of the 'breach in the wall', by which he meant the threat of heresy to the church. (J. I. Tellechea Idígoras, *Bartolomé Carranza, Arzobispo. Un Prelado evangélico en la Silla de Toledo*. San Sebastián, 1958, pp. 39–40.) The symbols of heresy were serpents, according to Pope Pius V in his Bull on the Rosary. Moreover, during his Toledan sojourn Carranza was critical of the sale of benefices (Ibid., p. 12). Some years earlier, this had been compared by the Papal Consilium to the Trojan horse (A. G. Dickens, The Counter-Reformation, London, 1968, pp. 97–9).

In spite of his reforming zeal, Carranza fell foul of the Inquisitor General and was accused of Erasmist tendencies. He was imprisoned for eighteen years. Not unnaturally, he died soon after his release in 1576.

It is significant that some of Carranza's supporters were patrons of El Greco: Diego de Castilla, the Dean of the Cathedral (Tellechea, Idígoras, op. cit., p. 66); Archbishop Quiroga (Boyd, op. cit., p. 76); Pedro de Salazar y Mendoza, the author of *Vida y sucesos . . . de D. Bartolomé de Carranza y Miranda*, Madrid, 1788.

The picture may refer specifically to the destruction of Carranza and, in general, to the prevailing mood of intolerance and antagonism to the spiritual reform movement.

The pose of Laocoön is derived from the *Wounded Gaul*, Museo Archeologico, Venice (F. Saxl, *Kritische Berichte Zur Kunstgeschichtlichen Literatur*. Leipzig, 1927–9, 1–2, pp. 86ff); that of his dead son is derived from a fallen *Giant*, Museo Nazionale, Naples. Both statues are from the Small Pergamene Altar, the Attalos dedication.

42. Detail of Plate 41.

43. Detail of Plate 44.

44. *The Immaculate Conception.* 1607–13. 347 × 174 cm. Toledo, Museo de Santa Cruz [89].

Painted for the Oballe Chapel in San Vicente, Toledo.

45. *The Adoration of the Shepherds.* About 1612–14. 320 × 180 cm. Madrid, Prado [28].

This painting was intended for El Greco's own tomb in Santo Domingo el Antiguo.

46. *St Peter.* About 1610–14. 207 × 105 cm. Escorial, Nuevos Museos [274].

It is possible that this picture and that of *St Ildefonso* (Plate 47) formed part of the Oballe Chapel decoration (see Plate 44).

47. *St Ildefonso.* About 1610–14. 222 × 105 cm. Escorial, Nuevos Museos [275].

See note to Plate 46.

48. *The Baptism of Christ.* About 1608–22 (finished by Jorge Manuel). 330 × 211 cm. Toledo, Hospital of St John the Baptist Extra Muros [46].

Pedro de Salazar y Mendoza commissioned this picture for the high altar of this hospital. The strange device whereby God the Father's gesture of benediction is addressed to the angel at the extreme left, who then directs his blessing to Christ, is derived from the *Celestial Hierarchy* of Pseudo-Dionysius the Areopagite (Wittkower, op. cit., p. 53).

1. *The Assumption of the Virgin.* 1577. Chicago, Art Institute

2. *The Purification of the Temple.* About 1568–70. Washington, National Gallery of Art

3. *The Purification of the Temple*. About 1570–5. Minneapolis, Institute of Arts

4. *The Martyrdom of St. Maurice*. 1580–2. Escorial, Nuevos Museos

5. *Allegory of the Holy League*. About 1576–8. London, National Gallery

6. Detail of Plate 4 .

7. *Lady in a Fur Wrap*. About 1577–8. Glasgow, Pollok House

8. Detail of Plate 4

9. *El Espolio (The Disrobing of Christ)*. 1577–9. Toledo, Cathedral Sacristy

10. Detail of Plate 9

11. *St. Peter in Tears*. About 1585–90. Barnard Castle, Co. Durham, Bowes Museum

12. *The Crucifixion.* About 1580–5. Paris, Louvre

13. *The Resurrection of Christ.* 1577–9. Toledo, Santo Domingo el Antiguo

14. *The Burial of the Count of Orgaz.* 1586–8. Toledo, Santo Tomé

15. Detail of Plate 14

16. Detail of Plate 14

17. *The Agony in the Garden.* About 1585–90. Toledo, Ohio, Museum of Art

18. Detail of Plate 14

19. *St. Jerome as Cardinal*. About 1595–1600. New York, Frick Collection

20. *The Annunciation.* 1596–1600. Villanueva y Geltrú, Museo Balaguer

21. Detail of Plate 20

22. *St. Martin and the Beggar.*
About 1597–9.
Washington D.C.,
National Gallery of Art

23. *The Baptism of Christ.* 1596–1600. Madrid, Prado

24. *St. Francis and Brother Leo Meditating on Death.* About 1600–5. Ottawa, National Gallery of Canada

25. *Cardinal Fernando Niño de Guevara*. About 1600. New York, Metropolitan Museum of Art

26. *The Crucifixion of Christ.* About 1600–5. Madrid, Prado

27. *The Resurrection of Christ*. About 1600–5. Madrid, Prado

28. Detail of Plate 30

29. *St. Bernardino*. 1603. Toledo, Museo del Greco

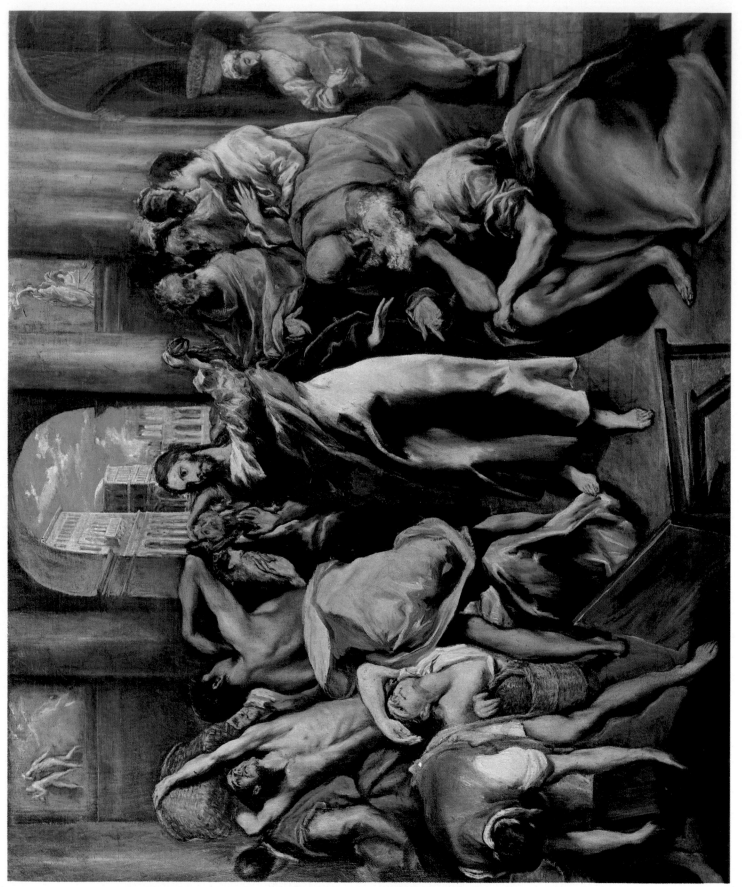

30. *The Purification of the Temple.* About 1600. London, National Gallery

31. *The Coronation of the Virgin*. 1603–5. Illescas, Hospital de la Caridad

32. Detail of Plate 30

33. *Fray Hortensio Félix Paravicino*. 1609. Boston, Museum of Fine Arts

34. *St. Ildefonso*. About 1603–5. Illescas, Hospital de la Caridad

35. *The Madonna of Charity.* 1603–5. Illescas, Hospital de la Caridad

36. *St. Jerome in Penitence*. About 1610–14. Washington D.C., National Gallery of Art

37. *The Vision of St. John the Evangelist: The Fifth Seal of the Apocalypse.* 1608–14. New York, Metropolitan
Museum of Art

38. Detail of Plate 41

39. *View of Toledo*. About 1595–1600. New York, Metropolitan Museum of Art

40. *View and Plan of Toledo*. About 1610–14. Toledo, Museo del Greco

41. *Laocoön*. About 1610–14. Washington D.C., National Gallery of Art

42. Detail of Plate 41

43. Detail of Plate 44

44. *The Immaculate Conception.* 1607–13. Toledo, Museo de Santa Cruz

45. *The Adoration of the Shepherds.* About 1612–14. Madrid, Prado

46. *St. Peter*. About 1610–14. Escorial, Nuevos Museos

47. *St. Ildefonso*. About 1610–14. Escorial, Nuevos Museos